20TH CENTURY MEDIA

1940s & 50s
THE POWER OF PROPAGANDA

was produced by

David West 👬 Children's Books
7 Princeton Court
55 Felsham Road
London SW15 1AZ

Picture Research: Carrie Haines
Designer: Rob Shone
Editor: James Pickering

First published in Great Britain in 2002 by
Heinemann Library, Halley Court, Jordan Hill,
Oxford OX2 8EJ, a division of Reed Educational and
Professional Publishing Limited.

OXFORD MELBOURNE AUCKLAND
JOHANNESBURG BLANTYRE GABORONE
IBADAN PORTSMOUTH (NH) USA CHICAGO

06 05 04 03 02
10 9 8 7 6 5 4 3 2 1

ISBN 0 431 15254 3 (HB)
ISBN 0 431 15268 3 (PB)

British Library Cataloguing in Publication Data

Parker, Steve, 1952-
20th century media 1940s & 50s: the power of
propaganda
1. Propaganda - History - Juvenile literature
I. Title II. Twentieth-century media 1940s & 50s
303.3'75'09044

Abbreviations: t-top, m-middle, b-bottom, r-right,
l-left.

Cover, 3, 5b, 7br, 9t all & br, 10bl, 13b, 15 all, 20r,
20-21, 22b, 26b, 27t, 28tr, 29ml & br - Popperfoto.
Cover br, 28l - The Art Archive/Eileen Tweedy. 4b,
5br, 6b, 7tr, 8b, 10-11, 14m, 18b, 20tl, 23br, 29tr -
Corbis Stock Market. 4tr, 16m - Mary Evans Picture
Library. 5tl, 11bl, 16bl & tr, 17tl, 19tr, 24tl - Topham
Picturepoint. 7bl, 18tl, 18-19, 19bm - The Kobal
Collection. 6l, 8t, 10m, 12 both, 12-13, 13tr, 14tl,
26tr - Hulton Archive. 9bl - The Art Archive/Imperial
War Museum WM. 11tr, 24r, 27b - The Culture
Archive. 17m, r & b - The Art Archive/D.C. Thoms
cpt. 21t - Associated Press/Topham Picturepoint. 21b
- Michael Ochs Archives/Redferns. 22tl, 23t & m -
The Advertising Archive Ltd. 25t - Vin Mag Archive
Ltd. 25mr - Leonard McCombe/Time Pix/Rex
Features. 25br - Frank Spooner Pictures. 27m -
Vogue/Condé Nast Publications Ltd.

*The dates in brackets after a person's name
give the years that he or she lived.*

*An explanation of difficult words can be
found in the glossary on page 30.*

20TH CENTURY MEDIA

1940s & 50s
THE POWER OF PROPAGANDA

Steve Parker

Heinemann
LIBRARY

CONTENTS

THRILL-PACKED STORIES OF THE FUTURE!

AMAZING STORIES

PRICE IN 1'6 GT. BRITAIN

ANC

When Two Worlds Meet

FUTURE FUN
Paperback books became big business during the 1940s. As an exciting yet inexpensive form of entertainment, their stories varied from inter-planetary war to historical romances.

OUTSIDE ACTION
During the 1950s television technology advanced at great speed. Cameras moved from the studio to cover outdoor events such as sports

THURSDAY, DECEMBER 31, 1903

2001 with incredulity and disgust

LIVING COLOUR
TV programmes in the 1950s were mostly broadcast in black-and-white. Viewers could only see colour pictures of their favourite TV stars in magazines.

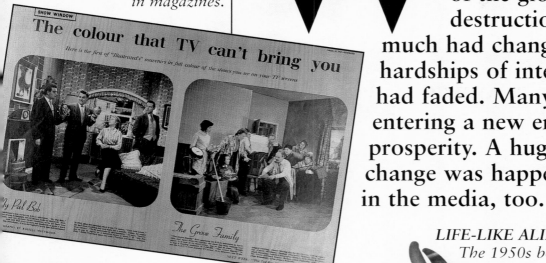

SHOW WINDOW

The colour that TV can't bring you

The Grove Family

WAR AND PEACE

In 1940, World War Two was spreading to engulf vast areas of the globe in death and destruction. Twenty years later much had changed. The horrors and hardships of international conflict had faded. Many regions were entering a new era of peace and prosperity. A huge change was happening in the media, too.

LIFE-LIKE ALIEN
The 1950s boom in science-fiction movies was partly due to continually improving special effects.

5

The mass media are the ways that we find out about news, views, events and opinions, and how we gain knowledge, information and entertainment. The media include newspapers, magazines, books, radio programmes, music and movies. Today's major mass medium is television. Before 1940, it hardly existed. By 1960, it had found its way into millions of homes in richer countries. The television revolution changed daily life for ever.

RAISING MORALE
During World War Two, many countries used the medium of radio to lift public mood, especially with comedy and cheerful songs. This is a 1941 studio scene from ITMA (It's That Man Again), a popular British programme.

KING OF THE WORLD

Today, global superstars come and go almost every week. But in the 1950s, they were few and far between. And even fewer were young. In January 1956, the voice of a young US truck driver, just turning 21 years old, shook the world with his first musical mega-hit, 'Heartbreak Hotel'.

MEDIA SATURATION

By the end of the same year Elvis Presley (born in East Tupelo, Mississippi and raised mainly in Memphis, Tennessee) had clocked up eight US No. 1 hits. Not only was his voice instantly recognized in almost every Western nation, his pictures were everywhere – on record covers, magazines, books, posters, in photographs, on television and in Hollywood movies. Nowadays it would be called 'saturation media coverage'.

RENE CHATEAU presents

ELVIS PRESLEY

KING CREOLE

KING CREOLE (1958)
In Presley's first series of movies, 1956–58, he usually played himself. He was a rough 'n' ready rising star of rock 'n' roll, adored by girls and admired by boys.

GUIDING STAR

Elvis was guided by his cunning manager 'Colonel' Tom Parker, who used every media opportunity to keep his star in the public eye. Parker also largely controlled Elvis's private life at the Graceland mansion in Memphis. But during the mid 1970s Elvis drifted into substance abuse and cabaret shows, and put on weight. He died in 1977.

Tom Parker and Presley.

THE COMEBACK KING

Elvis was soon worshipped as the 'King of Rock 'n' Roll'. In March 1958, he had to join the US Army, but that gave chances for more publicity and media coverage. In the 1960s, his records and movies were less memorable. Yet in his 1968 Christmas TV show he returned to his aggressive, sneering, hip-swivelling style. In 1973 his performance from Honolulu was seen live on television by more than one billion people.

THE RISE OF YOUTH CULTURE

Elvis triumphed in singing, music, movies, television, stage performance, and even in chat shows and interviews. He was also young. After the hardship of World War Two, young people of the 1950s had much more time and money. They had TV to watch and 'singles' (vinyl discs) to buy. These new developments helped Elvis to become the first multi-media megastar and gave young people a culture of their own.

MEET THE PRESS
The young Presley's relaxed style and easy-going humour made him entertaining at interviews.

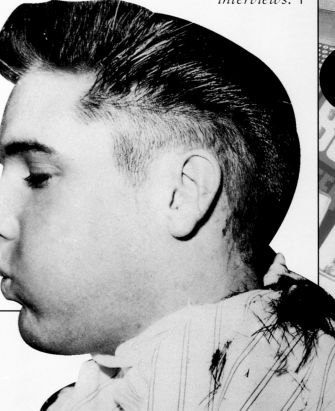

INTO THE ARMY
In March 1958, Presley had his 'long' hair cut short, army-style. It was yet another great photo-opportunity.

LOVE ME TENDER (1956)
Elvis's first movie introduced his smouldering good looks to the general cinema-going public.

FRONTLINE NEWS

Modern media can cover news live as it happens, via radio, television, and increasingly, the Internet. During World War Two only radio could bring instant reports. Most people kept up with events through newspapers, magazines and newsreels. The newsreels were filmed reports of recent events shown at cinemas, often before the main feature movie.

ERNIE PYLE
Pyle wrote about the personal lives of soliders and the terrors they suffered. He was killed with US forces in the Pacific, in 1945.

FINAL MORNING EXTRA
San Francisco Chronicle

U.S. AT WAR!
Japs Bomb Hawaii, Philippines, Invade Thailand, Malaya; U.S. Battleships Claimed Sunk; FDR Talks to Congress Today!

*USA AT WAR
In December 1941, American read about the Japanese attack on U. warships at Pearl Harbor, Hawaii. Thi brought the USA into World War Two*

PROBLEMS OF CENSORSHIP

When a country is at war, its media come under new pressures. It may not be wise to report all events fully and truthfully. If the enemy found out secret plans, this could put thousands of lives at risk. In World War Two the news media, especially papers and radio, followed government guidelines about what they should and should not reveal. Announcements, posters, songs and slogans encouraged ordinary citizens to support the troops abroad, and to smile while bearing hardship at home.

LEGENDS IN THE MAKING

Many correspondents became major media figures after the war. Radio reporter Edward Murrow moved to TV during the US anti-communist McCarthy era. Walter Cronkite became legendary anchor-man of CBS TV News (1962–1981). In Britain, 'Voice of the BBC' Richard Dimbleby described the horrifying Nazi gas chambers at Belsen. All were known for their sincere approach to uncovering the truth.

PERSONAL VIEW

Perhaps the most widely-read correspondent of the time was Ernie Pyle. He wrote, not about famous generals and glorious victories, but about the lives and deaths of ordinary US soldiers. He brought the terrible human tragedy of war back home to millions of people.

"Keep it under your hat!"

CARELESS TALK COSTS LIVES

POSTER CAMPAIGNS
Posters were pasted in public places such as main streets, squares and shops. Their slogans (sayings) urged people to help the war effort and to be aware of spies.

MATCHBOX MEDIA
Almost any item could be used to help win the war. These Japanese matchboxes raised feelings against Britain and the USA.

PROPAGANDA
To support a cause, information may be highly selected, distorted, or simply downright lies. This is propaganda. Each country in World War Two had its share. As part of German anti-British propaganda, US-born William Joyce broadcast on the radio in English, as 'Lord Haw-Haw'. In 1946, he was hanged for treason (betrayal of his country).

William Joyce laughed at his British listeners – 'haw, haw'.

CHANNELS GALORE

During the 1950s, furniture in millions of living rooms was moved around. No longer did people gaze into the flames of a fire, or sit around the piano or radio. There was a new focal point to look at – the television.

PETER PAN
This 1955 NBC show was first to attract 60 million-plus viewers. Peter was played by actress-singer Mary Martin, already a stage star in the musical South Pacific.

10

TV IN DISGUISE
Television sets were huge and bulky items. Many designs had opening doors or fold-away lids, to look like traditional furniture such as cupboards or desks.

AROUND THE WORLD

The new medium of television first took off in the USA, a rich country with a tradition of music, movies and entertainment. The first American coast-to-coast broadcasts were in 1951. Trends set in the USA, in technology and the types of programmes, quickly spread to other countries, especially Britain and Europe. There was cut-throat competition between major television networks for more viewers, to get more income from adverts (see page 13).

MR. VAN DOREN
ON THE AIR
10

CHEATS!

In the war to attract viewers, prize money on 1950s quiz shows reached gigantic amounts. But Herbert Stempel, a former champion on the leading show *Twenty-One*, revealed that some contestants were given the answers and told how to act. A huge outcry led to new laws against cheating on radio and television.

Stempel's successor Charles van Doren pretends to 'answer' a question.

BILKO AND BERLE

Phil Silvers as Sergeant Bilko (below) is still popular today. Milton 'Mr Television' Berle was the USA's first big TV star, in the comedy Texaco Star Theatre (1948–53).

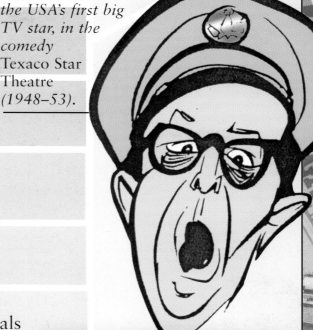

WE LOVE LUCY

The most popular show of the 1950s was the family comedy I Love Lucy *with Lucille Ball. Shown in more than 100 countries, some episodes attracted nine out of every ten TV viewers.*

SOAPS AND GAMES

An early success for TV was the soap opera. Its ongoing stories, and commercials for soap powders and other household goods, were designed to appeal to those watching at home during the day. From about 1954, audiences were gripped by big-money game shows, such as *The $64,000 Question* and *Twenty-One*.

CHANGING HABITS

Most early television was sent out live or recorded on movie-style film. From 1956, studio videotape meant that items could be recorded, edited and broadcast later. Daily habits changed as people sat to watch their favourite shows and, from 1954, eat TV dinners too.

LOOK
15¢ DECEMBER 28, 19
BABIES FOR SALE
our last black market
Tammany comes back—
the White House next

5th Annual TV Awards
coast-to-coast poll names
television's top stars and shows

LUCY and DESI
TV's favorite family

COLOUR TV

By the late 1950s, companies were testing colour TV, to replace black-and-white. Inside the set, tiny particles called electrons are fired in three streams called beams, from 'guns'. A magnetic coil makes the beams scan across the inner screen through holes in a mask. Tiny dots of substances called phosphors, in three colours, glow when hit by the electrons.

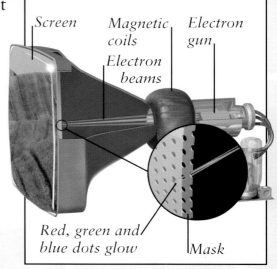

Screen *Magnetic coils* *Electron gun*
Electron beams

Red, green and blue dots glow *Mask*

NETWORK POWER

As the new medium of television mushroomed, so did its power. TV network bosses could decide a programme's content and approach. For example, a critical report about a politician could ruin that politician's reputation and career.

EXPOSED ON SCREEN

In 1954, US Senator Joseph McCarthy went on television to defend his anti-communist 'witch-hunts'. But his plan backfired. On screen for all to see, McCarthy showed himself as a scheming bully who used the media for highly personal, and often unjustified attacks.

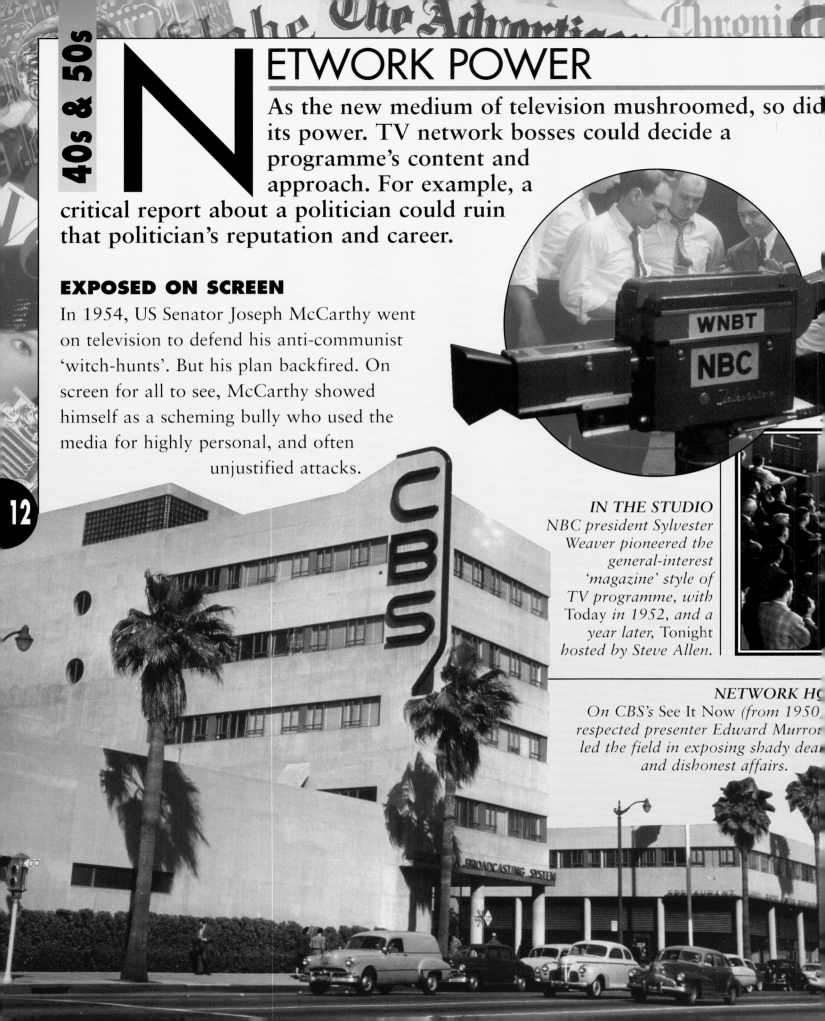

IN THE STUDIO
NBC president Sylvester Weaver pioneered the general-interest 'magazine' style of TV programme, with Today *in 1952, and a year later,* Tonight *hosted by Steve Allen.*

NETWORK HQ
On CBS's See It Now *(from 1950, respected presenter Edward Murrot led the field in exposing shady dea and dishonest affairs.*

SWEET SUCCESS

The power struggles between networks were especially fierce in the USA. The two main rivals were the Columbia Broadcasting System, CBS, and the National Broadcasting Company, NBC (owned by recording and radio giant RCA). From 1943, they were joined by the American Broadcasting Company, ABC. It was funded by Edward Noble, who had made his fortune from factories, which manufactured sweets and candy bars.

TV AT THE CINEMA
In the USA in 1946, there were 6,000 TV sets. Five years later there were 12 million. Some cinemas and theatres installed 'public' sets.

DIFFERENT SYSTEMS

The US networks competed for viewers and commercials, not always honestly. Across the Atlantic, the British Broadcasting Corporation, BBC, was funded by licence fees. It was more independent, with no need to attract advertising money. Many other European countries also started national TV stations.

SPONSORSHIP
TV was a huge medium for advertisers. This US Senate election (1958) was sponsored by a cake-making business.

LOOKING GOOD, SOUNDING GOOD
The first televised live debates between major politicians were in 1960. Richard M. Nixon and John F. Kennedy tried to persuade voters in the election for US President. Many TV viewers preferred Kennedy, yet radio listeners were persuaded by Nixon. This showed the importance of a person's visual image, as well as what he or she says.

Nixon (left) and Kennedy in one of their four live TV debates.

RADIO GOES MOBILE

The spread of television greatly affected radio during the 1950s. *Amos 'n' Andy*, one of the top-rated US comedy shows, lost more than half of its listeners between 1949 and 1952. Radio bosses needed to fight back. But how?

AMAZING INVENTION
Transistors were developed in 1947–48 at Bell Laboratories by (from left) John Bardeen, William Shockley and Walter Brattain.

ON THE MOVE

Television sets also began to use transistors. But the sets were still big and heavy. They needed a large aerial (antenna) to receive broadcasts, plus a supply of mains electricity. They had to stay at home. Radios became small enough to carry almost anywhere, for news and entertainment on the move – especially in cars, which were also mushrooming in numbers.

SMALLER AND SMALLER

Radio received an unexpected boost from a new electronic device, the transistor. This did a similar job to the valve (see diagram below), but it was much smaller and lighter. Also it needed less electricity. It was useful for all kinds of electrical equipment – especially radios. Engineers built smaller, portable, battery-powered receivers with transistors instead of valves. The first mass-produced transistor radio, from Sony, went on sale in 1952.

EASIER OUTSID
Radio reporters coul record their accounts on portable disc-cutter (tape-recorder almo anywhere, for broadcast later.

VALVES V TRANSISTORS

The transistor did much the same tasks as the thermionic triode valve. Its main job was to strengthen, or amplify, a varying pattern of electricity. But valves were big, heavy and hot, and they used lots of electricity. Transistors were smaller, lighter and cooler. They were also tougher and more reliable than the delicate valves.

Valve

Transistor

TARTAN TRANNY

A small, portable radio with transistors inside soon became known itself as a 'tranny'. This suitcase-type design with a handle copies the carry-alls or vanity cases of the time.

MADCAP FUN

A radio show needed no costumes, make-up or scenery. Compared to TV, it cost very little. So the medium of radio could afford to experiment with new ideas. In Britain, the BBC's *The Goon Show* (1951–59) set a tradition of zany humour and silly voices, partly borrowed from movie comedy such as the Marx Brothers. In turn, the Goons inspired TV shows of the 1960s, such as *Monty Python's Flying Circus*.

Goons (clockwise from top) Spike Milligan, Peter Sellers, Harry Secombe, Michael Bentine.

ON YOUR BIKE

By 1954, radios were small enough for bicycles. This version had a handlebar loudspeaker and crossbar batteries. However, road safety was a problem.

ON THE SPOT

Radio found other ways to compete with TV. Its news reporters could rush quickly to almost any location, such as the site of a disaster. It took much longer to transport and set up the large cameras and other machinery for television. So radio gained a reputation for being first with the news. There were also more radio stations than TV channels, with a wider choice of different programmes.

PAPERS AND MAGS

Newspapers and magazines survived the boom in radio in the 1920s, partly by using the new medium. They carried lists of radio programmes and times, features on radio shows and articles on the major stars. In the 1950s they did the same for TV.

AMAZING STORIES

Planet Earth's first science-fiction magazine Amazing Stories began in 1926. By 1950, it had a wealth of experience in imaginative ideas, gripping storylines and varied illustration styles. It was several years before movies and TV could catch up.

NEWS AND VIEWS

General-interest magazines such as Time, Fortune, Life and See 'fed off' other media, such as TV, radio and movies, with articles about them. This 1952 edition of See features a then up-and-coming movie actress called Marilyn Monroe.

RADIO TIMES

This 'listings' magazine began in about 1923 with the times of all BBC radio programmes. From the 1940s, it included television, but it kept its 'radio' name. The US version was TV Guide.

MORE MAGS

The print media of magazines and periodicals developed in two main ways, to compete with the broadcast media of radio and television. One of these ways was to 'feed off' the broadcast media by producing more publications. A flurry of new magazines and journals listed times and schedules, reviewed shows and went 'behind the scenes' to gather gossip and expose problems. Radio and TV fought back by doing the same to the print media.

Reuter's newsroom in London, 1951.

NEWS AND PRESS AGENCIES

It would be hugely costly for every newspaper, TV channel and radio station to send its own reporter to every news event. So news or press agencies attend major events and sell the information to the various media. Each paper, channel or station alters the details to fit its own approach. In 1958, two big agencies, United Press Association and International News Service, joined to form United Press International. This rivalled the Associated Press (founded in 1848) and London's Reuters (1851).

SPECIALIST MAGS

A second development was more specialized titles. Today there are magazines on almost every subject imaginable. But this was not so in the 1950s. So new publications began to explore narrow or single-interest subjects, dealing with just one topic in great detail. One of the pioneers was the USA's *Sports Illustrated*, founded in 1954.

MORE SPECIALIST MAGS

In a time of hazy television pictures, without slow-motion or action replay, *Sports Illustrated* attracted readers with high-quality photos and careful analysis of matches and performances. Many similar magazines soon followed, some specializing in just one sport. The trend spread to other interests such as gardening, cookery, movies and cars. Specialist children's publications also flourished, as popular radio and TV characters made their way on to the printed page.

LICENCES
A successful character, like a fairly amusing cat, could begin in any medium – comic, magazine, radio, TV or music. Other media could then buy a licence to adapt the character for themselves.

A T THE MOVIES

Before World War Two, Hollywood's movie-makers had come to dominate cinema. After the war they were still powerful. But they suffered from the spread of TV, problems linked to politics, and rising interest in films from other countries.

GUYS AND DOLLS
Sing-along musicals, here with Marlon Brando and Frank Sinatra, helped movie-goers to escape for a time into a fun world.

PROBLEMS, PROBLEMS

Cinema had been helped by newsreels – films of current events shown as small features before the main movie. With television, people could now watch the news at home. Also the anti-communist antics of US Senator Joseph McCarthy had spread from politics to entertainment and media (see page 28). Some of Hollywood's leading actors and directors, such as Orson Welles and Charlie Chaplin, were denounced as 'un-American'. As the arguments raged, Hollywood lost its grip on the movie business.

INSECT HORRO
The Fly (1958) was pa of a growing tren towards weird costumes ar special effects, for stories terror and science fictio

and disgu

ANIMATION

US animator Walt Disney's first major character was Mickey Mouse (originally named Mortimer Mouse), in 1928. Disney himself provided Mickey's squeaky voice. By 1940, the Disney corporation was producing a string of all-time great animated movies. *Fantasia* (1940) featured Mickey and other Disney characters set to classical music. *Pinocchio*, *Dumbo* and *Bambi* followed within two years. Later, Disney took to producing adventure films with human actors, such as *Treasure Island* (1950).

Bambi and friends, including rabbit Thumper.

MUSICAL FUN

However the big US studios continued to produce successful films, especially glossy musicals adapted from stage shows. They included *On the Town* (1949), *Oklahoma* and *Guys and Dolls* (1955), *The King and I* (1956) and *South Pacific* (1958). The musical movie had an added benefit. Its songs were released on record (vinyl disc), another media format which was rising in popularity. In this way, records and films helped each other to greater profit than either alone.

WORLD CINEMA

New film styles came from European directors such as Ingmar Bergman, Frederico Fellini and Francois Truffaut. Akira Kurosawa in Japan, and Satyajit Ray in India, also brought fresh ideas to the mainly Western movie business.

THE SEVENTH SEAL
In Ingmar Bergman's The Seventh Seal, *Death himself arrives to take away a knight, who challenges him to a beachside game of chess, to prove mankind's goodness.*

TRADITIONAL VIOLENCE
Director Akira Kurosawa adapted tales of Japanese life and tradition for epic movies such as The Seven Samurai *(1954).*

POPULAR MUSIC

During the 1930s, the growth of radio meant a dip in the sales of recorded music, which was then in the form of 5-minute grooved discs. The record industry hit back with two new disc formats, the long-player (LP or 33), and the single (45).

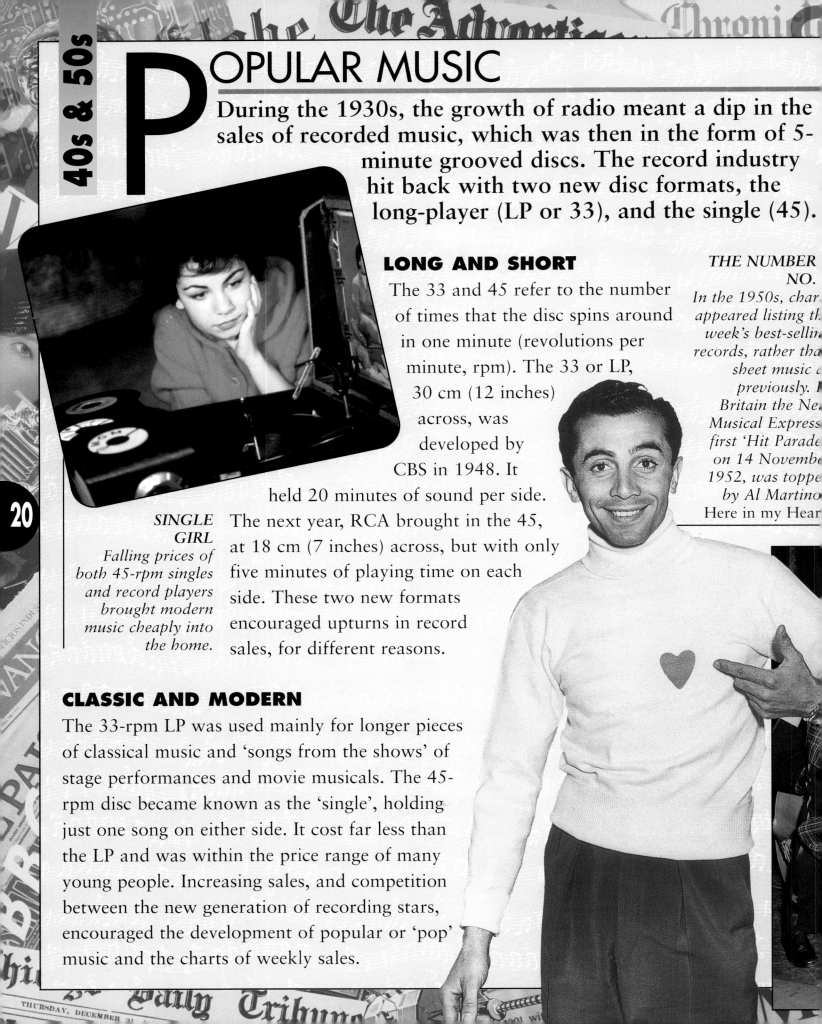

LONG AND SHORT

The 33 and 45 refer to the number of times that the disc spins around in one minute (revolutions per minute, rpm). The 33 or LP, 30 cm (12 inches) across, was developed by CBS in 1948. It held 20 minutes of sound per side. The next year, RCA brought in the 45, at 18 cm (7 inches) across, but with only five minutes of playing time on each side. These two new formats encouraged upturns in record sales, for different reasons.

SINGLE GIRL
Falling prices of both 45-rpm singles and record players brought modern music cheaply into the home.

THE NUMBER NO.
In the 1950s, char[...] appeared listing th[...] week's best-sellin[...] records, rather tha[...] sheet music [...] previously. [...] Britain the Ne[...] Musical Express[...] first 'Hit Parade[...] on 14 Novembe[...] 1952, was toppe[...] by Al Martino[...] Here in my Hear[...]

CLASSIC AND MODERN

The 33-rpm LP was used mainly for longer pieces of classical music and 'songs from the shows' of stage performances and movie musicals. The 45-rpm disc became known as the 'single', holding just one song on either side. It cost far less than the LP and was within the price range of many young people. Increasing sales, and competition between the new generation of recording stars, encouraged the development of popular or 'pop' music and the charts of weekly sales.

EELIN' AND ROCKIN'

Many established singers from the 1940s, such as Frank Sinatra and Bing Crosby, sang relaxed ballads or swing with big bands. Younger people, as always, wanted something different.

It arrived in the form of rock 'n' roll, which developed from a blend of many other musical styles such as blues, bouncy R&B (rhythm and blues), doo-wop, rockabilly and jazz. Rock 'n' roll was fast, noisy, exciting – and it annoyed older people. Its explosion into 1950s youth culture is described overleaf.

Alan Freed (1922–65).

THE DJs

Radio competed against TV by playing the latest music. Young people listened on their transistor radios, in bedrooms and cars, and on the beach, and bought the discs. In this way the two media, radio and records, benefited. Disc-jockeys (DJs) presented the music shows. US DJ Alan Freed worked in Cleveland, Ohio (1950–54) and then New York. He introduced black-origin music to a wide audience and invented the term 'rock 'n' roll'. His career ended in 1959, when he was accused of taking money for playing certain records.

WILD ROCK 'N' ROLL

Bill Haley and his Comets, formerly country-type musicians, popularized rock 'n' roll with hits such as Rock Around the Clock *(1954).*

PEGGY LEE

Rock 'n' roll was not the only popular music in the 1950s. Established singers, such as Peggy Lee, sold millions of records to older listeners. Peggy's biggest hits were Mr Wonderful *and* Fever.

NEW MEDIA MARKET

In 1950, there were no teenagers. By 1960, there were millions. That is, the word 'teenager' only came into use during the 1950s. It described young people with more time, money and freedom than ever before. They were a gold mine for the media.

POST-WAR FREEDOM

Teenagers were not just those aged 13–19. People who were no longer children, and also not quite established adults, had long lacked any identity as a group. Usually they were swept along by daily hardships, from work to war. But in Western countries, the 1950s were different. Living was easier. Parents were richer. Teenagers had access to mass media such as radio, TV, music, magazines and movies. They developed their own interests and created a whole new culture.

Calling All GIRLS

Largest Circulation Magazine For Girls .. more than ½ million

MAY 1945

COMICS · FASHIONS · THINGS TO DO · GOOD LOOKS · MOVIES · STORIES

TEEN MAGS
A fast-growing area of print media was the teenage magazine, with tips on make-up, fashion, hair styles and romance.

SCHOOL IS BORING
Movies and other media reflected the new culture. The Blackboard Jungle (1955) featured rock 'n' roll and rebellious pupils.

NOW **FOR THE FIRST TIME YOU CAN SEE**

COLUMBIA PICTURES Presents A STANLEY KRAMER PRODUCTION

MARLON BRANDO as

THE WILD ONE

with MARY MURPHY · ROBERT KEITH and LEE MARVIN

Screenplay by JOHN PAXTON
Directed by LASLO BENEDEK

NEW ATTITUDES

Teenagers became a new subgroup of the population, different from children and adults, with their own language and attitudes. The Wild One (1954) portrays reaction for its own sake against authority. Asked 'What are you rebelling against?' the star replies: 'What've you got?'

NEW ADS AND CUSTOMERS

New products and commercials were aimed at the teenage 'niche' of the market. In this version, success with fast cars and the opposite sex could be gained from a fizzy drink.

REBELS TO IMPRESS

Teenagers had cash from pocket-money, allowances and part-time jobs. They wanted to be different from their parents and rebel against traditions. They were at an 'impressionable' age when fashions and fads moved rapidly. Media bosses quickly realized that a whole new market was opening up for ever-changing programmes and products.

SHARED INTERESTS

Teenagers gathered in their own groups at coffee bars and soda parlours. They listened to rock 'n' roll on the jukebox, read magazines and discussed their own movies, books, clothes, cars and other important topics. They related to new young stars, such as Elvis Presley, James Dean and Marlon Brando, who dealt with teenage problems like ending school, starting work, relationships and a rejection of authority. The media-based youth culture established in the 1950s still flourishes today.

"Soup up" the conversation with this quick, refreshing lift!

extra sparkle helps. And the fun way to get it is with "7-Up"! Seven-Up gives you brand new energy. In just two to six minutes. And it leaves your thirst so fresh and tingly, you'll want a brand new drink!

nothing, nothing does it like Seven-Up!

7up

MORE FREEDOM

For centuries young women were expected to carry out chores at home, or to go out only with the family. But sales of washing machines, vacuum cleaners and other labour-saving gadgets soared. Housework took less time. Girls became more independent and could spend their money in many new ways.

Chatting at the 'milk bar'.

MEDIUM AND MESSAGE

Which is your favourite advert (commercial)? Often the advert itself is so clever, we forget which product it promotes. It may be easier to recall the medium – whether the ad is on television, at the cinema, in a magazine or newspaper, on radio or on a huge billboard poster.

NUCLEAR FAMILY

TV adverts for home-life items such as foods, drinks, appliances and soap powders showed a family of two parents and two children, one boy and one girl, all impossibly happy. This became known as the 'nuclear family'

CHOOSING THE MEDIUM

Television added yet another medium to the array of methods which advertisers use to reach the public. The fast-moving, fashion-conscious, powerful advertising business involves the manufacturers who make the products, the advertising agencies who produce commercials for them, and the media which bring adverts to public attention. In the 1950s, as now, advertising paid for much of a medium's output. Also the impression that an advert makes is greatly affected by the medium carrying that ad (see panel opposite). In the 1950s, TV was the new, high-tech medium and keen advertisers flocked to it.

THE AGENCIES

Advertising agencies specialized in making commercials for clients. Their media consultants decided which was the best medium to use, to promote each product.

MAKING A MESSAGE

Television brought images, sounds and actions right into people's homes. But producing TV ads cost huge amounts of money. Also, after a commercial was shown, the viewer's attention quickly moved on to the next item. Adverts in papers and magazines were more long-lasting and could have coupons or order forms. Also, as magazines became more specialized, advertisers could appeal directly to readers who were already interested in a product, rather than fleetingly to the general TV-watching public.

MAKING ITS PLACE

Advertisers quickly learned how to use costly TV adverts. Networks sold time for 'spot ads', where each region promoted its own local products and services during a commercial break in a national show.

SELLING A DREAM

Many adverts portrayed a dream-like perfect world. The suggestion behind this image was that, if you bought the car, you also obtained shiny big-city success and a rich lifestyle.

POWER COMPANIES BUILD FOR YOUR FUTURE ELECTRIC LIVING

MARSHALL McLUHAN

Canadian-born writer and teacher Marshall McLuhan published his first books in the 1950s. He became one of the first 'media gurus' with powerful opinions on the use and effects of different media. His phrase 'the medium is the message' meant that the form of communication – newspaper, radio, TV, poster – could be more important than the actual information it carried.

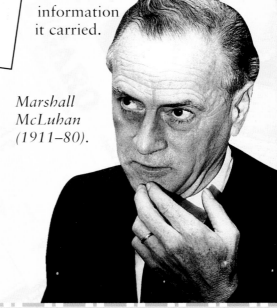

Marshall McLuhan (1911–80).

ON-LINE SHOPPING

In the 1950s, advertisers hoped that people could soon order goods by talking into a microphone linked to the TV and telecom network. But electronic shopping via computer did not became a reality until the 1990s – still without a microphone.

REAL LIFE PHOTOS

During World War Two, thousands of photographers on all sides recorded terrible scenes on the battlefields. Their pictures in newspapers and magazines showed the horror of war to people at home.

An early Polaroid Land camera.

PHOTO-JOURNALISM

One of the most influential photographers was French-born Henri Cartier-Bresson (born 1908). He rarely used indoor studio techniques and complex equipment. Instead he travelled the world with small, portable cameras, often working outdoors with black-and-white film rather than colour. His method was to survey a scene, compose a picture in his mind, and then wait for the 'decisive moment' when he could record it in real life.

NOT NEWS

Cartier-Bresson rarely attended big-news events. He wanted to capture the details of ordinary daily life, 'writing' with pictures in a documentary style, as a photo-journalist. In 1947, with Hungarian-American photographer Robert Capa (see opposite) and others, he founded Magnum Photos. It was an agency where photographers around the world co-operated to control sales of their own pictures in the international market-place.

MOMENT OF GLORY

In February 1945, US troops invaded the Pacific Japanese-held fortress island of Iwo Jima, in one of World War Two's bloodiest battles. Here, marines raise the US flag on the shore. Actually, this was a staged version organized by photographer Joe Rosenthal after the main battle. The image has become a symbol of the war, copied in movies and statues.

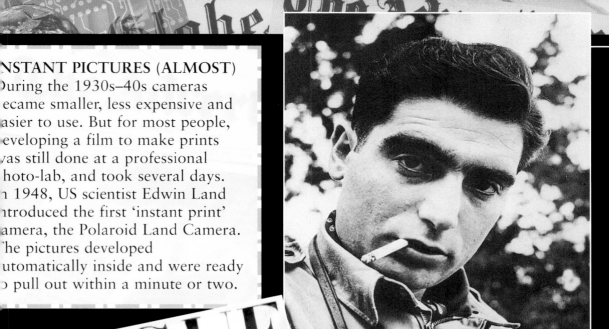

INSTANT PICTURES (ALMOST)

During the 1930s–40s cameras became smaller, less expensive and easier to use. But for most people, developing a film to make prints was still done at a professional photo-lab, and took several days. In 1948, US scientist Edwin Land introduced the first 'instant print' camera, the Polaroid Land Camera. The pictures developed automatically inside and were ready to pull out within a minute or two.

ROBERT CAPA

Capa (real name André Friedman) took many heart-stopping photographs of World War Two. He saw life and death in Africa and Italy, and waded ashore with Allied troops at Normandy, France on the D-Day Landings of 6 June 1944. Capa continued his war photo-journalism into the 1950s. In 1954 he was killed by a land mine in Vietnam, during the Indo-China War.

FASHION

Far away from wars and daily hardship, fashion photography developed into a 'high art', capturing the latest in clothes, styles, make-up and design. It could take days in the studio to produce one picture, as tiny details of lighting or the folds of a garment were adjusted time and again. The movement was led in the USA by photographers such as Richard Avedon and Irving Penn. Later Avedon also took portraits of celebrities. But he used frontal views, plain lighting and pale backgrounds to make them seem more 'ordinary'.

THE LATEST STYLE

Fifties fashion magazines such as Vogue and Harper's Bazaar had highly-posed, carefully-taken pictures on almost every page. They seem to be aimed at the rich and famous, but were bought by people who wanted to be rich and famous. The lack of background separates the image from reality and daily life.

BEST-OF PHOTOS

Among the specialist magazines that appeared in the 1950s (see page 17) were yearly or even monthly compilations of photos. This example is from a magazine of the best sports pictures of 1955.

THE COLD WAR

World War Two ended in 1945 amid great hopes for global peace and harmony. But new regional conflicts flared, especially in eastern Asia. And the two great superpowers, USA and USSR, entered a new struggle called the 'Cold War'.

援朝

援成奴隷國

7187

DAILY NEWS New York's Picture Newspaper 4¢ FINAL

STALIN DEAD

Malenkov F...

STALIN DIES

Daily Worker

Daily Mirror

STALIN DEAD!

Dictator Succumbs ...remlin

NEW YORK Herald Tribune City Edition

Stalin Is Dead

End Comes at Night 4 Days After Stroke

The New York Times. CITY EDITION

STALIN DIES AFTER 29-YEAR RULE: HIS SUCCESSOR NOT ANNOUNCED; U.S. WATCHFUL, EISENHOWER SAYS

STALIN DIE...

When long time USS... leader Josep... Stalin died, i... 1953, th... world held it... breath. Woul... the new leader... be more friendl... or could the East... West rift deepen...

STAND-OFF

The term 'Cold War' was devised by US media journalist Herbert B. Swope in 1947. The capitalist, freedom-loving USA and its friendly Western European nations faced the communist, state-controlled USSR with its Eastern European and Asian allies. These countries never came to a direct battle. Their 'Cold War' was fought largely through words and images in the media. Each superpower tried to outdo the other in military power, economic strength and the success of its political beliefs.

ANTI-COMMUNIST IMAGE
This United Nations-produced poster shows th... supposed dangers of communism in graphic form... A shadowy, rifle-toting North Korean soldie... looms over ordinary South Korean citizens wh... are being marched 'into communist slavery...

MENACE AT THE MOVIES

Propaganda is information which is highly selected or distorted to support a cause. Both West and East used it in many forms during the Cold War. In some Western films, villains had the facial features, sound-alike names and look-alike clothing of the communist enemy – even if they came from outer space! Stories in books described battles which were thinly disguised versions of the real East-West stand-off. In the East, roles were reversed. Western-looking baddies were portrayed as stupid, loud-mouthed and loose-living.

It Came From Outer Space *(1953)*.

LEAFLET DROP
US soldiers prepare rolls of printed matter to drop from planes over Korea, in 1950. The highly anti-communist message told about the dangers of the 'Red Menace' from communist North Korea.

REGIONAL WARS

In June 1950, communist North Korea invaded South Korea. The USSR supported the North. The USA, backed by the United Nations, aided South Korea, to prevent the spread of communism. The media, especially the new format of TV, showed harrowing scenes from Korean cities and jungles. Each side claimed it was fighting for the people there.

THE COLD WAR DEEPENS

The Cold War spread into many areas of media including movies, books, TV and radio programmes. A new form of mass communication was millions of leaflets, dropped from aircraft, telling the people living below which side they should support. The Cold War would continue into the 1960s and bring the world to the brink of nuclear attack.

McCARTHY'S CAMPAIGN
US Senator McCarthy's anti-communist 'witch-hunt' became too bitter and personal, and he was exposed on television (see page 12).

GLOSSARY

ANCHOR-MAN/WOMAN Host-presenter of TV or radio show, who introduces and links the various features and items.

BROADCAST MEDIA News and information sent out to many people – that is, broadcast – usually in the form of radio (electromagnetic) waves, as radio and TV programmes.

MCCARTHYISM Period in the USA during the early 1950s when people in politics, business and media were investigated for Un-American activities and communist sympathies.

PHOTO-JOURNALISM Conveying information such as a news story or report using primarily photographs with captions, rather than mainly written text with accompanying pictures.

PRESS A machine (printing press) that prints newspapers, books and similar items. Also a general term for reporters, journalists, interviewers and other people gathering information for the media.

PROPAGANDA Highly selected, biased or falsified information, which supports and propagates (moves forwards) a certain cause or campaign.

PRINT MEDIA News and information printed or otherwise put on to paper, as in books, magazines, periodicals, journals, newspapers and posters.

RADIO The general name for the sound-only medium which uses invisible electromagnetic waves sent out, or broadcast, from transmitter to receiver. 'A radio' is also the everyday name for a radio receiver or radio set.

STUDIO A large room where radio and TV programmes are made, or where an artist works. Also the general name for a large movie company or organization.

TELEPHONE 'Speaking at a distance', a system of changing spoken words or other sounds into codes of electrical signals and sending them along wires or cables.

VALVE An electronic device which looks like a small glass tube with metal parts (electrodes) inside. Valves have various jobs, such as using a very small, varying electric current to control a much larger current. Valves were mostly replaced by transistors, which were smaller and lighter.

WORLD EVENTS

- World War Two, Germany in Europe
- Germany invades Russia
- War rages in Pacific, Battle of Midway
- Churchill, Roosevelt and Stalin meet, Tehran
- Uprising in Warsaw crushed
- World War Two ends
- United Nations holds first major meeting
- India and Pakistan proclaimed independent
- Indian leader Gandhi assassinated
- North Atlantic Treaty Organization (NATO)
- North Korea invades South Korea
- Libya becomes independent
- UK: George VI dies, Elizabeth II succeeds
- USSR: Stalin dies
- Warsaw Pact nations (Eastern Block)
- South Africa leaves United Nations
- Crisis over Suez Canal, Egypt
- EEC or 'Common Market' formed, Europe
- Coup in Iraq, republic declared
- Castro comes to power in Cuba

TIMELINE

	HEADLINES	MEDIA EVENTS	MEDIA TECH	PERFORMANCE & ART
	•Churchill becomes British leader	•Press run stories of 'TV suicides' after bad news	•500th 'birthday' of printing press technology	•Fantasia: Disney cartoons and classical music
	•Japanese attack on US forces, Pearl Harbor	•Nazi leader R. Hess flies to Britain in secret	•Hans Haas pioneers underwater filming	•Noel Coward: Blithe Spirit
	•Gandhi put in prison in India	•Fleming, discoverer of penicillin, is media star	•US Report on Chain Broadcasting (FCC)	•Casablanca with Bergman and Bogart
	•German forces surrender, Stalingrad	•ABC network founded in USA	•SCUBA gear allows better underwater filming	•Oklahoma! musical hits Broadway
	•D-Day landings in Northern France	•US bandleader Glenn Miller lost in air mystery	•Early IBM computers used in radio calculations	•The Diary of Anne Frank
	•Atomic bombs dropped on Japan	•San Francisco: United Nations charter	•Arthur C. Clarke predicts telecom satellites	•UK: Cinema visits for a year peak at 1,630 million
	•Churchill coins phrase 'Iron Curtain'	•'Lord Haw-Haw' executed for treason	•Guild of British Newspaper Editors formed	•First Cannes Film festival, France
	•Un-American reports affect the movie industry	•Magnum Photo Agency founded	•Early types of transistor invented	•George Orwell publishes 1984
	•Allies airlift supplies to Berlin	•Milton Berle becomes USA's 'Mr Television'	•CBS develops 33-rpm 'long play' vinyl disc	•Key Largo by John Huston
	•Mao takes power in China	•Outcry over USSR test nuclear explosions	•RCA develops 45-rpm 'single' vinyl disc	•Disney uses real actors in Treasure Island
	•Wartime fuel rationing ends in UK	•First TV weather forecast aided by computer	•Estimated number of US TV sets exceeds 10 million	•The Goons develop their zany humour
	•Early colour TVs make big news in USA	•I Love Lucy, most widely shown TV show, begins	•First coast-to-coast TV broadcasts in USA	•CBS begins See It Now with Ed Murrow
	•UK: first 'Hit Parades' of best-selling records	•CBS radio network fails to make a profit	•First transistor radios	•Arthur Miller: The Crucible
	•Elizabeth II's coronation	•UK's great debate over commercial TV	•McLuhan: how electronic media mimic the brain	•The Seven Samurai by Kurosawa
	•US Senator McCarthy exposed on TV	•Sports Illustrated magazine begins	•TV dinners aid viewing	•First episodes of Sgt Bilko successful TV comedy
	•UK: Month-long national press strike	•NBC's Peter Pan sets record viewer number	•The Times (London) prints its first cartoons	•James Dean: East of Eden
	•Communist uprising in Cuba	•Elvis Presely explodes into the media	•IBM designs new logo	•Kerouac: On the Road
	•USA: Civil Rights Act and race riots	•Respected Vogue editor Edna Chase Woolman dies	•First space satellite, Sputnik (USSR)	•South Pacific, one of most successful musicals ever
	•'Ban the Bomb' anti-nuclear marches begin	•UK: LP (long-player) vinyl record charts begin	•United Press International formed	•Pop singer Buddy Holly dies in air crash
	•UK: BBC viewers fall by 70% as ITV starts	•US quiz and game shows hit by cheating scandals	•First silicon microchips	•Some Like It Hot, since voted all-time great movie

INDEX